I0484696

KEEP-IT-SIMPLE GUIDE

TO

INTERNET MARKETING

Diana Clark

15 Easy Steps
To Building your Business Online

Editorial Director: Kathleen Mix
Published by: CJP CONSULTANTS INC.
Cover Design: Diana Clark
Production and Composition: Diana Clark

ISBN - 1451554095
EAN - 139781451554090.

ACKNOWLEDGEMENTS

My thanks to Maria and Angii for their great
Publishing Challenge, to Kathleen for her
meticulous work, and to Charlie Page who
inspired me to start my Internet journey.

MORE **KEEP-IT SIMPLE** GUIDES....to follow

KEEP-IT-SIMPLE GUIDE TO INTERNET MARKETING

15 Easy Steps to Build Your Business

Introduction

1. **Personal Branding - Creating Your Internet Identity**   **1**

2. **Simple Website Power**   **7**

3. **Creative Writing – or Not?**   **13**

4. **Photos and Videos - a Picture is Worth a Thousand Words!**   **17**

5. **"Tweet, Tweet" and all that Social Media Jazz**   **21**

6. **Flirt with the Search Engines – Google, Yahoo and Bing**   **29**

7. **Host Your Own Radio Show – For Free!**   **33**

8. Advertising - Does Adsense
    Make Sense?   35

9. Build Your Client Relationships –
    Know, Like and Trust   39

10. Keep In Touch with your
    Clients Online   43

11. Expand and build your
    Virtual Team   47

12. Multiple Income Streams for
    Your Business   49

13. Formulate your Formula!   51

14. Rinse and …. Repeat   53

15. Learn the Lingo - Glossary
    of Internet Terms   55

INTRODUCTION

"Eat the Internet elephant one bite at a time."

Diana has taken the mystery out of building a business online with this Keep-It-Simple Guide to Internet Marketing.

The guide explains how to set up a simple business website, with photos, graphics and videos. Host your own free blog radio show and build loyal clients and customers with the Know, Like and Trust factor and keep them coming back for more!

She has spent the last year researching and implementing the basics of Internet marketing for her company CJP CONSULTANTS to help offline clients expand their businesses online.

Her background as a business and education consultant, professor and writer has led her to design this step-by-step process for the individual or business owner who needs to know how the pieces of the Internet advertising puzzle fit together. Diana has also created an Internet Resource Center at:
www.cjpmarketingonline.com.

This guide is dedicated to those beginning their Internet journey, those who have begun and are overwhelmed, and those seeking to share their business, hobby or passion with a global audience.

There is life after the 50 hour week and you have the unique skills and abilities to do this! Take it one step at a time and you will "eat the Internet elephant."

Chapter 1

PERSONAL BRANDING
Online and Offline

The most important part of branding is the image
you portray. Developing a likeable personal brand
is essential for success.

If you want to rise to the top of your particular
arena, you need to be able to sell yourself to your
potential customers. Think about it. Would you
rather do business with a person who smiles and
comes across as friendly - or with one who is
indifferent and lacks passion? This is not rocket
science – remember the last time it happened to
you in the grocery store or the shopping mall or
waiting for "Customer Service." The first
impression a potential customer receives is from
you. Make it a good one. How can you
accomplish this?

2. Consider what your target audience needs and wants, and then identify the value and the experience that you can deliver to meet those needs and wants.
Communicate in ways that reach into the hearts and minds of your target audience and connect with their core values and deepest desires.

3. The personal branding process is about having self-awareness of your strengths and talents and experience, and then letting everyone know about them!

It is about giving a clear impression of **who** you are, **what** you value, and **how** you can be counted upon to act.

Your branding statement must provide a clear, concise view of your unique set of strengths and tell **why** you can do it better than anyone else. You need to be able to state clearly **how** you are different from everyone else, what services you offer that make you unique and sets you ahead of your competition. Consistency is one of the keys to building a strong personal brand. Be aware of being consistent in every interaction you have, both in what you say and how you respond to the communication.

Chapter 1

PERSONAL BRANDING
Online and Offline

The most important part of branding is the image you portray. Developing a likeable personal brand is essential for success.

If you want to rise to the top of your particular arena, you need to be able to sell yourself to your potential customers. Think about it. Would you rather do business with a person who smiles and comes across as friendly - or with one who is indifferent and lacks passion? This is not rocket science – remember the last time it happened to you in the grocery store or the shopping mall or waiting for "Customer Service." The first impression a potential customer receives is from **you**. Make it a good one. How can you accomplish this?

One: Become an expert source. Learn as much as you can about your business and keep learning. Knowledge is power and generates dollars in the bank.

Two: **Become a great communicator**. Research shows that communications skills are the top determinants for upward social and professional mobility.
Say what you mean and mean what you say!

Three: Draft a marketing plan for yourself annually, and review quarterly. Include specific goals, strategies, action steps, and a timetable.

Four: **Develop an "elevator speech."** Within the time that it takes an elevator to travel one floor - about 60 seconds - be able to deliver a succinct description of what you do, how you do it differently, and the benefit it provides. That is part of your business first impression!

Five: **Build your online Rolodex/email list**. Make new business contacts and stay in touch with them. Most people with powerful brands have powerful friends.

Six: When **networking offline**, balance your individual style with clothing that will appeal to those you are trying to impress.

Seven: **Practice good business and social etiquette** - send handwritten notes. On line, send personal emails to your clients and customers –set up an electronic greeting card delivery for birthdays or special events.

Eight: Give something back. Giving your time, talent, and money to charitable causes is a brand-builder especially when it complements your brand strategy. Find a cause that excites and motivates you!

Your personal brand is one of your greatest business assets. Invest as much time and effort into it as you do into branding YOURSELF - in the end, if you can't sell yourself, you will find it nearly impossible to sell your product and services.

Key Ingredients in Branding

Personal Branding can be the most influential tool for success in your self-marketing toolkit. You can identify, package and sell who you are to build a personal brand that results in business growth, influence, and income. Here are three key things you need to develop a strong personal brand:

1. Be clear on **your** personal strengths, talents, values and core area of expertise. Understand how you connect best with people.

2. Consider what your target audience needs and wants, and then identify the value and the experience that you can deliver to meet those needs and wants.
Communicate in ways that reach into the hearts and minds of your target audience and connect with their core values and deepest desires.

3. The personal branding process is about having self-awareness of your strengths and talents and experience, and then letting everyone know about them!

It is about giving a clear impression of **who** you are, **what** you value, and **how** you can be counted upon to act.

Your branding statement must provide a clear, concise view of your unique set of strengths and tell **why** you can do it better than anyone else. You need to be able to state clearly **how** you are different from everyone else, what services you offer that make you unique and sets you ahead of your competition. Consistency is one of the keys to building a strong personal brand. Be aware of being consistent in every interaction you have, both in what you say and how you respond to the communication.

Establishing a **Professional Brand** is absolutely critical to long term, sustainable business growth. In an overcrowded marketplace, if you are not standing out, then you are invisible! **Branding** your products and services will give you an edge over your competition and enhance your value to your target market.

PERSONAL BRANDING ONLINE

All the same principles apply. You will need a professional website that captures the visitor's attention. Your website needs to reflect your personal brand, your logo, your picture - whatever set you apart from the crowd!

A means for your clients and customers to communicate with you on line. We will be discussing adding a Blog (web Log) to your main site as this is where you can really establish your personal brand or that of your company.

Your Unique Selling Proposition – what makes you special!

Exposure on Google Search Engine so that your clients and potential customers can find you.

A smiling image, maybe a video or audio of you, good email response, quality of goods and services offered. You will be promoting yourself, utilizing all the principles discussed above. Now let's take the next step.

Visit me at www.cjpmarketingonline.com for more information on **Personal Branding**.

Chapter 2

SIMPLE WEBSITE POWER

Now that you are comfortable with your personal branding strategy, it is time to plan the next step.

Having your own website today is as essential as your business card used to be! It establishes you and your company's products and services in the global economy.

WHAT TYPE OF WEBSITE DO I NEED?

Option 1 – your Business Card website.
In today's economy, many individuals and small businesses have a very small or non-existent budget for advertising and marketing. Fortunately, there are several options for creating a simple site. Here are a couple of suggestions:
There are several companies on the Web where you can create your initial business card site: Weebly.com, Intuit.com or Vistaprint.com.
This can be a good place to start if your time and budget are limited.

You can sign up for a free account and start creating your page right away. All of these companies provide step by step instructions. Additionally, they offer paid hosting and design services if this is your choice. Before you start - think about our company name, the colors and design and the content you want to include. Don't forget to solicit your kids' friends and/or local college students for extra help and advice for a minimum investment!
This will provide you with a simple site to get you started.

Option 1 is recommended as a simple step to create your "your business card" online and then to move to Option 2 for your main website.

Before you do – ask yourself:
What do I need to create a good website?
Is it clear and easy to read ?(don't overdo it!)
Is the content relevant and interesting?
Is it specific?
Can your clients and customers communicate
with you through this medium?

Think about the purpose of your website.

How do I incorporate my personal branding?
Is it a corporate business?
Is it to promote your passion?
Is it to sell your goods and services?

If you need some inspiration, go to Google Search
and find sites in your niche – particularly those
ranked on the first page, and see how your
successful competitors do it!

Option 2 - Your own website using **Wordpress**

Wordpress is great for creating a website because
it allows you to make changes and additions
yourself with very little technical know-how.
Wordpress.com has some excellent tutorials,
however this can be a time consuming process
until you get the hang of it and most business
people prefer to outsource this.
.

I went through the whole process in order to be able to establish a knowledge base for my clients and provide a comprehensive service for them.

Keep-It-Simple Tools:

You will need your own registered domain name, webhosting company and email responder - these are the steps to take:

1. Register a domain name – buy the .com name (your address on the Internet). The fee for each name is $8 -10 per year.

Tips for your domain name:

> * Keep it short and easy to remember
> * Make it relevant to your business
> * Include location for a local business

The well-known names in this field are: www.domain.com, www.namecheap.com, www.godaddy.com

I have used Domain.com as it seems the easiest to navigate, but have a look and see which you prefer. My focus in this is to make it as simple as possible – this is uncharted territory for most newcomers to the Internet.

2. **Choose a web hosting company** – they take care of your site on their massive Web servers and provide technical support which we need when we have our own sites. The best known are:
www.hostgator.com, www.bluehost.com, they charge a monthly fee which is usually under $10 per month.

3. **Sign up for an autoresponder** - these companies accept your customers' email addresses from the sign up box on your website (called an opt-in box). The main reason for having a website is to communicate with your potential customers and provide the goods and services needed. To send unsolicited email is SPAM, so your customers need to confirm their subscription to your mailing list.

   The established companies are:
www.aweber.com and www.getresponse.com. I use Aweber and they provide excellent support and video tutorials. The cost is under $20 per month

4. **Build a Wordpress Site** - I know that sounds scary, but a Wordpress site is easy to manage once you have the basics! Go to YouTube and Google for how- to videos or there are many free or inexpensive online training programs.

If you prefer, you can outsource this for under $100 for a simple site. For more tips on Wordpress training and suggestions visit me at www.cjpmarketingonline.com

5. Start a Blog

Go to Blogspot.com and set up a free blog with a name that follows the theme of your Wordpress site. – this can be your newsletter, chat room and an opportunity for extra information and weekly updates linking to your main site .

If this all sounds too much to do – don't worry - you can outsource the tedious technical tasks once you are comfortable with how the whole tangled Web fits together.

Keep-it-Simple hint – decide what you need for now and take action – you can always add the "bells and whistles" later.

Remember -the goal is to have your own website! Visit me at www.cjpmarketingonline.com for more **Keep-It-Simple** resources!

Chapter 3

CREATIVE WRITING – OR NOT?

Now that you have your website – we need to fill it with interesting content!

If you love to write – no problem for you! However many people need help in this area. This is where the **Keep- It- Simple** steps come into play.

There are so many good free or inexpensive options. If you need to become an expert on your clients' products or services, do a Google search on your website subject and you can look and see what your competition is doing– try some of the large companies and you can gain inspiration from their copywriters.

Don't copy them, but you can see what they are doing successfully.

To research articles on particular topics, go to

www.ezinearticles.com, and www.goarticles.com.

These are the article directories where you will submit your own material later as part of your marketing efforts. Notice the Author's Bio Box where you will see a link to the relevant website. This is where you add your information and website address. Most articles are 400-600 words.

Type in your category of interest and there you are! Do not copy word for word – Google's computers do not like duplicate content – but this will give you inspiration. If you just hate to write content - don't worry – here are your solutions – let the writers do it for you.

Two sites which many people use are:

www.99centarticles.com and www.elance.com

Go to the website and ask for bids for your project. Be specific about the content or article you need. From there, writers will make bids on your project and provide you with writing samples so you can get an idea of their skill level.

It is important that you find a freelance writer that matches your content and style. If you are looking for a copywriter, do not hire someone who specializes in technical writing. Sometimes it is better to pay a little more as quality is more important than quantity.

The more you are willing to pay per article, the more bids you will get from qualified writers who know how to entertain and inform your Website visitors, so that they come back for more!

Hopefully you will find one or more writers with which you can build a relationship and work with them on your writing projects in the future. It is worth the time and effort to start building the virtual team you will need in the future.

It is very important that you focus on your strengths in your business and think in terms of what you can and should delegate!
No one can do it all, and there are only 24 hours in a day. Whether you are a consultant, a small business owner, a lawyer or a general contractor,

you need to think in terms of how do simplify your business online.

Keep- It -Simple Solution – outsource it! You now know what sort of content is needed having done your research and understand the process!

For more resources – visit me at www.cjpmarketingonline.com

Chapter 4

A PICTURE IS WORTH A THOUSAND WORDS

There are many excellent free or very inexpensive resources to add photos and videos to your website.

Photos and Images

You will need photos or your company logo for a profile or bio and you may have original photos you want to upload. If you are looking for specific images, these are the resources I use and recommend: Google Images, (Check copyright if you use them) www.istockphotos.com, www.stockxching.com.

They are royalty-free and will not create a copyright problem for you.

Videos

YouTube is an excellent resource to find videos for your site. However you may wish to make your own with a Flip Camcorder or outsource it. Go to Google search – "promotional video makers." YouTube is also full of how-to videos on all aspects of website development marketing, if you have the time to explore them.

You can have your own YouTube channel at no cost to help promote your brand or your clients' products and services. This is very powerful way to capture a global audience, as well as a useful tool for a small local business to showcase their goods and services.

There are many video tutorials on how to upload video to your website. Do a Google search or visit me at www.cjpmarketingonline.com for more resources I have used and can recommend.

They are also great training tools for specific

tasks for your virtual team (See Chapter 11).

Photo sharing sites

A Keep- It -Simple way to upload and download photos is from Flickr.com. You have the option to publish the photos to the Web if you wish, which is another tool to link to your website. Most people use Flickr for personal use, but it can also have a business application . There are other options too, such as Photobucket.com. Check them out and see which works best for you.

Image and Video sharing sites.

Jing.com is free software for capturing images and short videos for sharing. You can also upgrade to their Pro version for more options.

Google has a photo sharing site named **Picasa.**

SQUIDOO

Squidoo.com.

This is a great opportunity to create another simple website with graphics and videos to link to your main website. It takes about an hour maximum to build once you have decided which components you wish to add.

For more information about the value of Squidoo visit me at www.cjpmaketingonline.com

Chapter 5

TWEET, TWEET AND ALL THAT SOCIAL MEDIA JAZZ

Some of my clients ask me – why do I need Social Media? The **Keep-It-Simple** explanation is that it is the fastest growing segment in Internet Marketing – CNN, Fortune 500 companies, media celebrities and the 80+ million people who are doing it to increase their customer base cannot be wrong!

These are the steps to take:

Twitter for Business

Open two accounts at Twitter – one for personal and another for your business. The next thing you will want to do after your profile is set up correctly is start to attract "followers". If you have business contacts or an email list that are already using Twitter, invite them to follow you.

Put your Twitter address in your emails, on your websites and blog asking people to follow you. You could even put it on your business card, so that you can gather followers from offline as well. Don't be shy; tell everyone you meet about your Twitter page. Make it sound exciting and let everyone know that you will be sharing important updates, great tips and information with them if they follow you. You may be surprised to find out that almost everyone will click the follow button just to see what you're up to.

Establishing your business

Twitter Backgrounds

A custom Twitter background is very important as it shows followers that you are serious about your business and about helping your followers on Twitter. It just adds that extra bit of professionalism to your image. The background on your Twitter page defines your personality and the quality of your business.

If you want to save time and get a hot looking background created, the best way to go is to hire a designer to create one for you. If you want to do it yourself, there are many pre-made Twitter backgrounds available that you can edit using Photoshop.

Your custom background design can vary depending on your business, but always have a picture of your face with a smile, your name and your company name, website address and logo (if you have one).

Building a list of Twitter followers

Let the world know that you are on Twitter! You need to spread the news that you're on Twitter. You will want to include your Twitter ID in your email messages, post blogs and on your websites. That way, everyone will know that you're using Twitter.
Tweet good content. Often – daily not weekly!

Believe it or not regularly updating your tweets will help you drive more traffic to your site. Avid Twitter users like people who post tweets regularly. If you want to gain active followers through your tweets, you will want to set up a schedule for posting and do your best to stick to it.

You will also want to make sure that you reply to the tweets addressed to you. I don't recommend that you stay on the site all day or spend long hours tweeting away your time. Just pick a good time once or twice a day and log in.

If you have a mobile device, all the better because you can sync it up with your Twitter account.

Here is a little checklist that you can keep handy:

- Let everyone know that you're on Twitter.
- Send tweets regularly.
- Retweet good content. (Pass it on to your following)
- Reply to the tweets addressed to you.
- Pay attention to the kind of Tweets you're sending.
- Make the tweets personal, but businesslike .
- Most of all, **build good relationships**.
  Remember each message can only be 140 characters so it's short and sweet
  for Tweets!

Twitter Tools

Twello
Twitter's Yellow Pages which allow you to link with people and businesses around the world. Add your Twitter business page/profile
and you and your business are connected globally.

Social Oomph

Our next tool is Social Oomph – formerly known as Tweet Later. This tool lets you schedule your tweets, auto-follow people who follow you and send them a DM (direct message) automatically and much more.

Social Oomph offers a free service but there is also the option to upgrade for even more features. Let's look at the main benefits of using a tool like Social Oomph:

Automating your Tweets

You can schedule tweets to go out automatically at a time you set. This is great if you aren't able to send important tweets because you have other commitments. It only takes a few minutes to set up a program that you can use to automatically post your prepared tweets.

This can be handy for business if you are preparing a product launch or an even such as a teleseminar/webinar and want to keep your followers up to date about it but don't want to be manually posting to Twitter.

You can select the option to auto-follow people who follow you and send them a DM at that time automatically. This is a great way to introduce yourself and make friends quickly. You can add a short message in the DM that states "thanks for following me. I'm an expert in ABC so please let me know how I can help you."

Just be certain that your message doesn't go over 140 characters. You probably don't want to send them straight to your website or else they'll smell you as just another 'sales' person right away.

Maximizing Your Twitter Traffic

Re-Tweeting

Now let's talk about getting your Tweets spread even further and increasing the chance of meeting even more people by using 're-tweets'.
Re-tweeting is a common practice on Twitter where you'll re-post someone else's tweet that you like and you think your followers will like.

With this method, you take the original twitter message someone else has posted, and rebroadcast that same message to your followers. To do a re-tweet, simply type in RT at the beginning of your tweet and then a @ before the original tweeters username followed by their original tweet.
Now Twitter will let you click the Retweet button on the Twitter website which will set up the RT function automatically.

Facebook for Business

Again - open two accounts at www.facebook.com a personal one and a Facebook Fan page for your business. Facebook has over 62 million active subscribers and still growing. The fastest growing segment is the over 35's.
It is no longer just for the 18-25 year olds!

The same building of relationships applies to all Social Networks but one of the excellent features of Facebook is that it allows you to promote your goods and services in a more comprehensive way – add videos, pictures and even games and applications which can be great in attracting people to your page – don't be afraid to think out of the box – be creative but don't oversell – make it interesting and you will attract a lot of targeted traffic.

LinkedIn for Business

Sign on at www.linkedin.com and set up your business profile. LinkedIn is particularly good for local business to business presence and networking.

Keep-It-simple expansion step for Social Media marketing:

Sign up for a free account at www.onlywire.com sign up to join over thirty other social networks, add their button to your website and submit your content to all of them with just a click! It takes a little time to set up but it is worth it in the long run. For more helpful hints - visit me at www.cjpmarketingonline.com

Chapter 6

FLIRTING WITH THE SEARCH ENGINES

GOOGLE, YAHOO AND MSN/BING

Google is the largest Search Engine – multi-million searches a day for everything you can imagine.

How can Google et al work for your business?

The goal here is to have your website ranked highly on the first page of Google Search in your category. Why not go to Google.com and explore a little? Type in something you are looking for, a product or a solution to a problem and see what comes up. See who is successful in their ranking on the first page – it may give you some inspiration!

So what questions or queries do your potential customers have, or what product are they looking for?

Your first goal is to provide the answers on your website and to provide Google with every opportunity to rank you high on the first page in your category or "niche."

Your second goal is to have the customer click on to your site, join your mailing list and purchase goods and services you offer. If he or she finds useful information and/or a solution to their problem, they will buy from you.

Search Engine Optimization

Keep- It- Simple explanation – these are the methods you or your web team use to get visitors and potential customers to your website.

The tools we have discussed in this Internet **Keep-it-Simple** Guide are the basics which will allow Google to visit the site, evaluate and rank it.
Your website, blog, radio show, videos ,photos and interesting information all help to provide "Google juice" – the ingredients which help propel your website to the first page Bear in mind this is done by computers, not people so it needs to be a methodical step-by-step process. Websites are like good wine- they need time to mature.

Having said that, there are methods to propel your site to Google very swiftly (usually in a less competitive market) but that is the subject for another **Keep-It-Simple** guide! Keep adding more content on your blog, new photos and videos and you will get there. It works. I've done it and so can you!

Open free email accounts with Google, Yahoo and MSN. You will need them as you expand your relationship with the Search Engines.

Google is also a wonderful resource for expanding your horizons on the Web. It is a library, shopping mall (Froogle), encyclopedia, problem solver, language translator, global phone book - just type into the Search Box and bingo!

Google is also your research tool for your client's website – to find what their customers' needs are and what problems your product or service can solve for them.

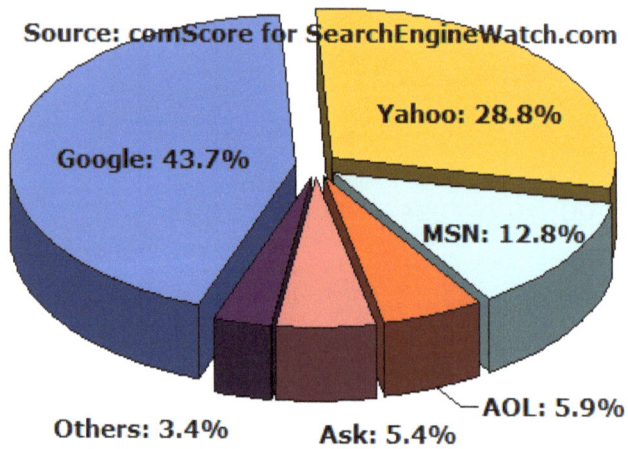

Source: comScore for SearchEngineWatch.com

Yahoo: 28.8%

Google: 43.7%

MSN: 12.8%

AOL: 5.9%

Others: 3.4%

Ask: 5.4%

As you can see, Google has the largest share of the Search market and is growing larger every day.
It is worth investing some time becoming familiar with Google – it has so many features which will be valuable to you in your understanding of successful Internet Marketing - this **Keep-It-Simple** guide is designed to give you an overview of the many processes involved.

For more resources on Search Engine Optimization please visit my website:

www.cjpmarketingonline.com

Chapter 7

HOST YOUR OWN RADIO SHOW FOR FREE!

No **really -** you can do this! For those with stage fright - remember this is a wonderful way to expand your business and you don't have to look your best. You can interview guests and colleagues, have someone interview you and you can interact with your listeners on the paid version.

Go to www.BlogTalkRadio.com and sign up! They offer training and support for up to a one hour broadcast. You can advertise your website in your Host Profile, and of course talk about it on the show.

If this is not for you right now - you can still make an audio MP3 in the privacy of your own home and record it to put on your website. Go to www.Audacity.com and download the free software. This gives you a recording studio online. It is amazing! You will need headphones and microphone for your desktop computer if it is not already built in. Allow a little time to figure this out and maybe enlist some help but once you get the hang of it – it is magic!

Podcasting
Keep-It-Simple explanation - Personal on Demand Broadcasting – once you have your recording, you can add it to your website using Podpress and your visitors can click on it and hear your message.

Webinars
Webinars are online seminars are usually on a particular topic and are educational. You can include the features and benefits of your business along with it, of course.
Some are purely audio with a choice of computer or phone listening while others include visual and audio components. One of the main companies to use is www.GotoWebinar.com. They offer a 30 day free trial and a reasonable monthly fee if you are planning to use them for a series of events. Email invitations are sent to your customer list and they can sign up to attend. Webinars are a very effective way of keeping in with your clients and

customers on line – giving them great information and promoting a product and/or service you offer.

Chapter 8
ADVERTISING – DOES ADSENSE MAKE SENSE?

Now that you have your site up and running with good content, it does make sense to add some advertising in most cases. If you have a corporate site then your ads will reflect your products and services - however if you promoting your own goods and/or services then why not add some extra revenue streams?

Making money with Google Adsense is at cost to you – these are ads from other companies that pay you when your visitor clicks on them for further information.

Setting up an Adsense Account

Go to Google com and sign up for an Adsense account. You will need to include your website address – they provide a step-by-step process. You can target ads in different geographic locations if you wish and customize the colors to match your website design. You submit your application for approval. Google usually responds within 3 days – this is an electronic process. **Keep-it-Simple** hint – check your spam folder – I found my first approval there .
Transfer Adsense to your website and you are in business. When your visitors come to your site and read your content if they click on an ads you get paid a few cents. Probably not enough to retire on - but it helps cover the small business costs of your site!

Keep-It-Simple warning – DO NOT click on the ads yourself or encourage your colleagues to do so – the computers at Google will "slap" you – they hate fraudulent clicks.

As your business grows, you may want to allocate an advertising budget to Google Adwords. Those are the ads you see on the right hand site of the search pages – check them out. You, as the advertiser, pay per click anywhere from 5 cents to $3.00 for very large and competitive markets. You can limit your daily budget with Google.

How does my site show up on Google?

A potential customer types in a question, "how to" a problem they need to solve e.g. "cure for acne" "Ipod instructions", "Cheap divorce" – you get the idea!

The title, content and solutions should be very specific on your site in your category and if it matches the query – up comes your site! Type in some Google searches of your own and you will see that the sites that show up on the first page are the most relevant to your query.

This is the **Keep-it-Simple** explanation of what is called Search Engine Optimization and the secret to your success. Sounds easy but it needs to be very precise!

Article Marketing

As we discussed in Chapter 3, if you submit articles to www.ezinearticles.com and www.goarticles.com, you can increase your exposure on the Web – Google loves good articles. In the Resource Box below your article you can add your website so that visitors who liked your information will click on to your site. Check out the sites and vast array of topics covered. If you hate to write– follow the suggestions in the Creative writing chapter. There are other advertising avenues to explore but this is the subject of another **Keep-It-Simple** guide.

The **Keep-it-Simple** Key to Marketing

1. WHO are your clients/customers?
2. WHERE do I find them?
3. WHAT problem does my product or service solve for them?
4. HOW is my company unique?
5. WHAT am I selling?

If these five questions are answered on your website – you are on your way to a successful business. The old saying "Find out what the customer wants and provide it to them at the right price" is still just as true for business online.

Chapter 9
BUILDING RELATIONSHIPS
KNOW, LIKE AND TRUST!

People buy from people that they Know, Like and Trust. (The KLT factor)

Its all about establishing trust and credibility

Where do you buy your clothes from?
Who services your car.?
Who is your dentist, doctor or attorney?
I'm sure you chose these people because you trust them.

Why do people buy goods and services online?

Convenience – Purchasing is easy. You don't even have to leave your home.
Price and Quality – They offer products at a discount to online merchants.
Preference – They offer products for which they know a demand exists.
Payment Terms – They offer easy payment options by credit card.
Customer Service – Toll-free number and email support.
Return and Refund policy – usually money back guarantee.
Sales Promotions – Offer special promotions and discounts on a regular basis.

Yet, many online businesses fail. Why?

Because:

They have failed to build relationships!

Helping a client/customer in need is the best opportunity to build a relationship.

Encourage them to comment on your blog – get their feedback – build their trust!

Word of mouth is powerful even in the Internet world - chat rooms and online forums attract likeminded individuals to learn from and share advice with each other.

Give value to your clients and then they will buy from you.

This is not the usual face-to-face offline relationship. It is just as critical that they become familiar with you and your company, hence the use of photos, videos and radio shows as communication tools.

The "heavy sell" technique will not work for long term business success – **solve their problem** and they will buy from you.

I am sure you have heard of the old 80/20 rule - 20% of your customers are responsible for 80% of your business. You will want to build a list of loyal customers who will come back and use products and/or services again. These loyal customers are also the ones who will recommend you to others – the most powerful way to grow your business online.

Reward their loyalty with discounts
Or special offers – give them helpful information and let them know you value their business!

A successful business relationship is not unlike a good marriage – it takes time to build a solid foundation and to mature into a solid partnership.

Your loyal customers will also give you feedback on how you are doing if you ask for it. This is very valuable information and means you can continue to provide what they need and want. You can add a Comments page or Poll to your website if you wish and use your Blog to keep your customers informed of updates and useful information.

It is the personal touch which makes all the difference – who would you rather buy from … a person you know or a complete stranger?

That is the challenge online –building and maintaining the relationship with your customer.

For more hints on building client relationships - visit me at www.cjpmarketingonline.com

Chapter 10

KEEP IN TOUCH WITH YOUR CLIENTS ONLINE

This is where we start to put the components together from the previous steps.

This is what you have accomplished so far:

Set up your Personal Brand
Established your Website
Free Advertising
Photos and Videos
Hosting Your Own Blog Radio Show
Google, Yahoo and Bing to bring traffic to your website

Twitter, Facebook and LinkedIn communicating with your clients!
Webinars

Pretty impressive – huh? Give yourself a big pat on the back!
You already know more about Internet business than 90% of your colleagues except those who are Webmasters!

The next step is the importance of keeping in touch with your existing clients/customers and continually building new ones!

Blogging

It is a good idea to set up a Blog – **Keep-It-Simple** explanation – a weblog similar to a newsletter online – which you update on a weekly basis at least, and daily if your time schedule permits. As your business grows, you will be able to bring in more help with some of the Web tasks which will free you up to expand.
Blogger.com is Google's free blog – simple to set up. Choose a name for your blog that is similar to your website or use your own or a pen name for a personal brand.

If you need some ideas, use Google Search and find blogs that pertain to you or your client's "niche". For example "Make Money online" blogs

Gardening blogs, Cosmetic Surgeon blogs – see how they do it, note your likes and dislikes on their style and design. This will help you with your content and layout.

Your blog will enable you to get feedback from your customers and clients, allow you to keep them updated with new products and services and give them useful information to help them as part of your customer service to them.
You can add articles, videos and webinars of interest and they can be archived so your new customers will have a wealth of information to attract them to return to your website.

Tweeting

Just a short message daily - 140 characters - 80% informational 20% promotional – remember these are personal relationships you are building and keeping! Now you have set up your Onlywire account, all Social Media messages will be sent with the click of the mouse! The value of Onlywire is that you will cover as many of the Social
Media sites that you choose apart from the "big three" we have discussed.
If you are still skeptical about Social Media marketing as a corporate tool – check out Dell's

multimillion profits from their following on Twitter!

Newletters

We talked about your autoresponder– the email company which takes care of your customer list and emailing confirmation to the subscriber from the opt-in (sign up) box on your website.
Both Aweber and Getresponse offer newletter e-distribution to your list and a choice of templates (designs). This could be a monthly special for all your subscribers and helps to build your list.

Visit me at www.cjpmarketingonline.com

Chapter 11

EXPAND YOUR BUSINESS
BUILD YOUR VIRTUAL TEAM

As your business grows, you will need extra help!
If you have an offline office with staff, then you
can train them on the tasks you need to delegate.
However, some of the tasks are very specialized
and it is better to outsource to experts in the field.
The good news is that you have gained a working
knowledge of how business online operates
and you can choose the right person for the right
job!
These are some of the people you may need as you
expand.

Virtual Assistant – He/she can be in the U.S or anywhere in the world. You will need someone to co-ordinate your projects if you do not have an offline staff. I recommend you use Skype (free phone calls on your computer) to communicate with your online folks. Ask for a resume and try them out on a few specific tasks before making a job offer! There are many excellent people out there but it needs to be a good match for you and your specific needs.

Graphic Artists

Go to: www.forum.digital.point.com and post your project – ask for samples of work before you decide on who will do the best job for you or offer a prize for the best design or graphic on your project.

Promotional Video maker:

www.mypromovideos.com

Wordpress Editor

Go to: www.scriptlance.com and again ask for a bid on your project. These folks will build your website for you but you will need to be specific about what you need – that's the reason to learn about Wordpress and perhaps build one website for yourself so you understand the process before you outsource. **SEO Experts -** Visit me at www.cjpmarketingonline.com for more information

Chapter 12

MULTIPLE INCOME STREAMS FROM YOUR BUSINESS ONLINE

If you own a business, run a company, are a dentist, lawyer, have a car dealership or own a Laundromat   you need to establish a professional website. This will give you the opportunity to gain and retain more customers or clients, and therefore increase your income in today's tight economy.

If your goal is to set up your own business online and make money from it, there are several ways to accomplish this:

Sell your own product or service – do you make jewelry or have special family recipes to share? Do you keep tropical fish or have a natural remedy for weight loss? The possibilities are limited only to your imagination. There are millions of people searching for products and services every day on Google.

Selling other people's products and services – this is called affiliate marketing. Many major companies such as Amazon, Overstock, Clickbank.com have affiliate programs selling thousands of products –
check out their websites.

Set up a site related to your passion or hobby and share it with others around the world through your social media network you have built on Twitter, and Facebook. Do you
love crafts, expensive watches, video games, or cars? There are so many options.

Advertising revenue from your site -
Google Adsense or Adwords if you have
a budget for Google. Keep building your customer lists, build trust and loyalty with them and they will buy from you.

Chapter 13

FORMULATE YOUR FORMULA!

As you can see, you have built quite an impressive presence in cyberspace! There are many other bells and whistles you can add - but if you just follow all the steps in this **Keep-it-Simple** guide you have done more than most of your competition and can see the process working!

The last step is:

Formulate Your Formula - **Keep-It-Simple explanation** – make yourself a Mindmap and see where you are. You can design one that relates to your business.
(Go to FreeMind.com for the free software.) This is a simple example and a great way to visualize you progress and to plan your future projects.

Then you RINSE AND REPEAT!

For more information please visit me at:
www.cjpmarketingonline.com

Chapter 14

RINSE AND REPEAT!

Keep updating your website – with Wordpress that is fairly easy to do – keep Tweeting and Blogging and coming up with creative ways of pleasing your customers. Keep sending articles to Ezine Articles, doing radio shows and webinars and why not write a book? I did!
Remember, if your website is active and growing – so is your business.

Use all the amazing free resources on Google and don't forget YouTube for video tutorials – that helped me when I got stuck on a particular "how to."

If you are advising your clients on internet marketing – keep supplying them with helpful hints and information and the latest trends and developments.

I do hope I have saved you some time and confusion with this first **Keep-It-Simple** Guide – I certainly wish that I had something simple when I started my business online!

Please contact me at www.cjpmarketingonline.com and let me know!

Chapter 15

LEARN THE LINGO – A GLOSSARY OF INTERNET TERMS

AdSense - Google's advertising program for website owners (which Google calls publishers). AdSense ads are displayed on your site by Google based on the keywords appearing on your site. Google will pay you an undisclosed amount of money every time someone clicks on one of the ads being displayed on your site.

AdWords - Google's Pay-Per-Click advertising program.. Advertisers can bid on certain keywords and Google will display text ads on the search results page when people use that keyword to search.

Advertorial - A special type of ad that looks and sounds like an article, but is in fact an ad. Very few publishers will allow advertorials.

Autoresponder - A computer program that allows email to be sent to a list of subscribers on a scheduled basis. Email messages can be written once, and then delivered to each person who subscribes on a schedule you decide.

Blog - The term blog stands for Weblog. A weblog used to be a way for website owners to communicate with a small group of people. Today, blogs have become much more as website owners sell products, offer opinions, syndicate their content, and more with blogging software and services

Character Spacing - The number of letters and numbers making up one line of information.

Classified Ad - A small text ad, usually appearing in an ezine. Classified ads are generally three to five lines deep by 65 characters wide.

Content - This term simply means the words on your website but has taken on a new meaning as syndication is becoming more widespread. See syndication for more detail.

Conversion Ratio - Generally understood to be the percentage of people who come to your site and take the action your site asks them to take. Example- If 2 out of every 100 new visitors buys something, your conversion ratio for sales is 2%. Understanding this percentage is important because it tells you if your site is causing people to take the action you want them to take, be that subscribing to an ezine or buying something today.

Copywriting - The process of writing the words for a web page.

Co-Registration - This is where a company helps you build your mailing list by getting their visitors to register for your mailing list. Some companies do this for a living and you pay them by the subscriber, usually anywhere from 15 cents to $1.50 per subscriber.

CPA / CPS - CPA stands for Cost Per Action, and CPS stands for Cost Per Sale. These are arrangements where the advertiser pays the publisher only when a particular action (like a visit to a website or a sale) occurs. Most publishers don't like CPA advertising because it's hard to verify that the action took place.

CTR (Click through rate) - CTR is the number of people who click on your pay per click ad compared to the number of people who view the ad. Example: If 1000 people see your ad and 100 click the ad, your CTR is 10%.

Display URL - A pay per click term meaning the web address (URL) you want people to see when they see your ad. In most cases it can be different from the Target URL, which allows you to use an ad tracker without people seeing the long ad tracker link.

Directory - A categorized list of information. Yahoo is a directory where Google is a search engine.

Double or Verified Opt-in - The process of having subscribers confirm their desire to receive your information by clicking on a confirmation link sent to them via email. This second step ensures that the person verifying their subscription made the original request.

Download - The process of saving a file to your personal computer from a website. On Windows PCs it usually involves clicking a link with the right mouse button. On a Mac it usually involves holding down the shift key while clicking a link. In both cases, you then choose where on your computer to store the file.

Ebook - An electronic book, suitable for reading on a computer monitor. Some eBooks come in EXE format and can only be viewed on a Windows computer. The new standard is to create eBooks in PDF format, which can be viewed by any computer, or (in most cases) printed.

Editor - A person who contributes content to an online publication or webpage. Unlike a webmaster, an editor is usually responsible for only certain pages on a website and can generally only add or edit contributions they make to the site.

Ezine - (Electronic magazine) Much like an offline newsletter, ezines exist primarily to deliver information to their readers. They support the costs of publishing by selling advertising. Like their offline counterparts, ezine publishers usually don't write the articles they include in their ezine, but instead use the articles of others to create their ezine content.

Follow Up Series - A series of email messages delivered over time to prospective customers who have requested further information.

FTP - Stands for File Transfer Protocol. A computer program that allows transfer of files from your personal computer to a web server. Using FTP is the most common way to transfer web pages to a web server when you create a web site. Transferring files is accomplished using a program called an FTP program.

Forum - An online gathering of people with a common interest. Forums are run using a forum script (software) that allows the moderator to approve messages to display as well as displaying messages in subject order.

HTML - Stands for HyperText Markup Language, HTML is the code that causes web pages to display text and pictures.

Joint Venture - Usually an agreement between a person who owns a mailing list and a person who wants to promote a product where the list owner mails an ad for the product and earns a percentage of all sales.

Lead Generation - The process of getting people to ask for more information about a particular product. The term lead generation is often used in the MLM business, and sometimes used to describe the process of co-registration.

Moderator - The person who controls which messages are displayed on a forum. The moderator is usually an expert in the subject of the forum he or she moderates, and helps keep inappropriate postings off the list of messages forum members see. Inappropriate messages are usually messages that contain foul language, hate, or blatant advertising.

MP3 - A type of audio file that can be heard on personal computers or MP3 players. Most teleseminars are recorded in MP3 format for later listening.

Niche Marketing - Selling products and services to a group of people with a common interest. Although the name "niche marketing" is heard often these days, marketers have always focused on "niches" in order to make sales.

Opt-in - The process of a reader requesting more information from a site. The reader is opting to be included on a mailing list, hence opt-in. All legitimate email marketers use an opt-in process to ensure that their selling messages go only to people who want to receive them.

Opt-In Subscriber - Ezines are only sent to people (subscribers) who ask for the ezine by emailing a request to receive the ezine or filling out a form on a website where the ezine is offered. This opt-in process is important because it ensures that the ezine is delivered to people who are interested enough to request it. Ezines are not mailed to non-subscribers, and have nothing to do with bulk email or spam.

Opt-out - The process of sending email to people and telling them they must ask to be taken off the list in order to stop receiving email. Opt-out is a bad marketing technique and most often associated with spammers.

PPC (Pay Per Click Advertising) - A type of advertising in which the advertiser pays only when someone clicks on his or her ad. Google AdWords and Overture are the best examples of pay-per-click advertising, although some website owners now offer PPC to advertisers as well.

PDF - Stands for Portable Document Format. A trademark of the Adobe Company, PDF files can be read by any computer that has the free Adobe PDF reader.

Publisher - The person or company who produces an ezine. In the case of a large ezine, there might also be an editor who is responsible for the content of the ezine. Most ezine publishers also edit their ezine.

RSS - RSS stands for Really Simple Syndication and is one format that websites use to syndicate content. To see content that is syndicated you need a special program (called an aggregator) or you can view it on certain websites designed for this purpose.

Sales Letter - The words on a webpage that convince visitors to buy products.

Script - A set of commands that cause a computer to act in a particular way. There are many scripting languages (such as PERL and PHP) and these languages are the "code" that programmers use to create programs.

Search Engine - A site that finds other sites or files based on keywords. Google is a search engine where Yahoo is a directory.

SEO - Stands for Search Engine Optimization. This is the process of changing your webpage so that it is more attractive to search engines. When a webpage is properly optimized it is shown more often and in a higher ranking on the search engine results page.

Shopping Cart - A script or service that allows website owners to have autoresponders, create order forms, create a catalog of products, manage client lists, deliver digital products, run an affiliate program, and more - all from one site or using one piece of software.

Solo Ad - An ad that is mailed to a list of ezine subscribers on its own. Since no other ads are included in the email sent to subscribers, the ad can be said to be running "solo".

Subscriber - A person who asks to join a mailing list.

Syndication - The process of displaying content from one site on another site. This is usually accomplished by adding several lines of JavaScript to the HTML code of the web page where the content is to be displayed.

Target Marketing - The process of selling goods and services to a group of people who have a common interest. This term is identical to niche marketing.

Tracking Ads - The process of putting a tracking link in your ad. A tracking link is one that, when clicked, will record the click and redirect the reader to the site you want them to see.

Target URL - (Also called the destination URL) A pay per click term meaning the website where people will go when they click on your ad.

Teleseminar - A phone call where many people can listen and (usually) several experts discuss a particular topic. Teleseminar calls are often recorded and provided to customers in MP3 format for later listening.

Thank You Page - The page a customer is sent to upon successful payment for a product. The thank you page is often where links are provided to download the product purchased.

Upload - The process of transferring a file from a local computer to a web server. Uploading is most often done using software and a process called FTP.
Verified Opt-in - See Double Opt In listed above.

Web Host - A company that rents space on a web server to customers who want to have a web page.

Webmaster - The person who runs a website from a technical standpoint. The webmaster is usually the person who creates and uploads the webpages to the web server and maintains control over the entire site.

WYSIWYG - Stands for What You See Is What You Get and means that the page that is printed or displayed will look identical to the one that is composed.

This Glossary is reprinted by permission of Charlie Page, Owner of **Directory of Ezines.com**

www.ingramcontent.com/pod-product-compliance
Lightning Source LLC
Chambersburg PA
CBHW040839180526
45159CB00001B/240